How to Stop Smoking and Start Living

by Francesca Hepton

ISBN: 978-1-9999126-6-6

How to start being the best you
How to start living your dream

First published in 2016
by Babili Books
a division of Babili Services Ltd
UK company

CONTENTS

Introduction

The birth of How to...

I found myself constantly looking up "How to..." on the Internet, from how to cook a perfect roast, to how to do squats, how to grow potatoes, how to install a floor - it's all on there. The Internet is such a fabulous source of information. Everyone is sharing:

- their experiences

- their own personal beliefs

- what works for them

- what doesn't work for them

- what drives them

- what scares them

The list is endless and admittedly there is a lot of unsubstantiated gunk out there too that we have to wade through with a logical head. Therefore be warned! Do not believe everything you read just because it is in black and white doesn't mean it's true, just like everything you see in adverts isn't true:

1

For example: eating a chocolate bar with the intimation that it is a sexual act, a source of hedonism, isn't going to make you look slim like the model who is actually eating or pretending to eat the chocolate on the advert or feel happy like the model who is making the money doing the *choco-porn thang*.

Use your common sense.

In my no-nonsense books, I have listed the best ways to help you find out how to give up bad habits or gain new good ones:

How to...

Save Money
Stop Smoking
Give up Drinking
Be Happy
Look Young

The books complement each other, because if you want to give up bad habits, be healthier and look your best, these are all intertwined. One has a domino effect on the other.

A simple way of looking at THE DOMINO EFFECT

If you quit smoking you'll feel healthier, you'll look better, you save money and be happier!

Here are the plus sides:

No more aging of the skin	looking healthier
No more feeling rundown	feeling better
No more burning money	feeling happier
No more ruining your health	looking younger

It works with any of the categories in my books:

Example 1: Save money, you feel happier, when you're happier you are more positive so you look great and because you feel so much better you are more likely to do stuff and want to get rid of any bad habits.

Example 2: Get fit. When you get fit you naturally lose the bad habits like smoking, and drinking and any other drugs you might be addicted to. You definitely save money and you are all round much happier in yourself.

I wanted to help people get on the path of life they wanted to be on, instead of trudging along the path they were forced on, ended up on or just found themselves on. If you are able to keep your choices open, then you keep the door to freedom open. I wanted to share my research and insight with others to help them get back onto their path, reset their internal compass and be the best version of themselves.

PLUS I am sure being happy, fit and healthy is something you want to do and that is a big point I really cannot emphasize enough. Your drive is what will power all the changes.

YOU WANT TO DO IT

By studying the self, the different "egos" that govern our moods and thoughts (Egolosophy©), we can master how we react to certain "cues", certain "triggers". That is also an essential factor in breaking bad habits. Another major factor in addition to your drive and the recognition of the triggers is your ability to change. Change can come in the form of a change in circumstances or changing your life situation or simply wanting a change because you are tired of being a slave to your bad habit.

CHANGE – DO SOMETHING NEW

It's not giving up, it's doing something different.

Try something new, do something else. You've done the smoking thing. That's old hat now. Gone. Passé. Yesterday's news.

There is a lot of literature out there advocating how to give up smoking: hypnosis, patches, gum, exercise…. you can use all of these "aids" or just one or two. Whatever suits you and your character and lifestyle. This guide does not promise a magic formula, it will get your mind-set ready for stopping, it will show you reasons why you should stop (aside from the glaringly obvious one of CANCER!) and help you keep you going after you've stopped so you never want to make smoking a part of your life again.

In addition to your improved health and all the money you'll save, I will show you how much time you will gain. Since everybody knows about the detrimental effects smoking (tar and nicotine specifically) can have on their immediate and future health but they are still smoking, I thought I would emphasize what you could do with all your new spare time once you've given up. As a bonus factor, when you give up, you don't feel so tired meaning you actually *want* to do more and *can* do more!

My personal experience is dotted throughout my books as an example of what can be achieved by simply giving up bad habits like smoking. It is not just about the cigarette, it is about a way of life. I've gone from a girl who had it all to a girl who threw it all away to a girl who came fighting back from the dead and took hold of her life again.

From being an alcoholic smoking 15 to 20 cigarettes and sitting 10 to 12 hours at the computer working to pay off my lazy bum partner's debts, I am now a happy yoga fanatic and jogging freak, fit at 40+, own my own house, writing books, making videos, running my own business and feeling satisfied.

I have brought up 2 fantastic young men and learnt how to speak 3 other languages - and that turnaround dear reader was just in two years. And it all started with giving up smoking (and drinking).

Yes it is amazing what can be achieved in such a short space of time – admittedly the raising the children thing is an on-going project – just imagine where you want to be and start to make the change.

Why I want to change: (write your answer here):

_____

_____

Take a small piece of card and write down where you want to be in life. What is your dream. One the other side write down: "I can do this when I stop smoking." Keep the card in your pocket to remind you each time you put your hand in there that you have a dream. You want to change. You are ready to change. Stopping smoking is just the first step to realizing the life you really want.

If you want to change your life either by giving up a bad habit, staying fit healthy and happy - tuck into my book(s) they won't break your bank but they will give you your life back. Put yourself first. Invest in yourself.

Important points:

- Get out of your comfort zone and don't look back.
- Cut your shackles and set yourself free.
- Don't see it as giving up; see it as starting something new.
- Take charge of your life.
- There is so much great stuff to do out there!
- Don't miss out on your amazing life.

1. YOU'RE IN CHARGE

A lot of us seem to forget that we are actually in charge of our own life. We decide what we do, just like when our body tells us to eat when we are hungry. Your brain and body work off the information and experiences given to them. If you feed your body junk it will be unhealthy. If you feed your mind positive thoughts and experiences you are more likely to be happy, and so on. Think about what you expose your body and mind to. You are in charge of this.

Nature vs. Nurture

You can explain a lot of your make-up and behaviour through genetics, but you can "nurture" your life and the way you think in order to become more positive and make changes: think of WHAT you want, WHO you want to be. You are not set in stone. If you want to change, you can.

Examples of what YOU might want: You want to learn how to swim. You want to live in Iceland. You want to work part-time and spend more time doing taekwondo. You don't care if you don't have the biggest house on the street or the flashiest car or that your trousers are from the supermarket instead of a boutique with a brand name, because ultimately, here is the biggest "want" people have,: You want to be happy.

Don't forget to be you

Sometimes because we are so busy being the person people and society are telling us to be, the only time we feel like "ourselves" is when we indulge in our habit like smoking. It's your "peace" time, your "time out" your "me time". But it's really just the easiest and most convenient habit to fit into the day. If your passion is scuba diving you can hardly do that in your coffee break. But cigarettes are small and convenient, you pop them in your bag or pocket and they only take around 10 minutes to smoke.

But is it a habit you really want to carry on with?

You should really only include things in your life that you want to do. Don't do something just because your mother or father did it, or because your neighbour does, or a Kardashia-whoever does it. Do it because it feels right to **you**.

THE FIRST STEP: IF YOU DONT WANT TO GIVE UP, DON'T GIVE UP – do you want to give up?

First and foremost decide if YOU think it is a bad habit. If you don't, and I mean 100% don't think it is a bad habit, there is no point even trying to start the giving up process. Like I said at the beginning, you wanting to break a bad habit is the power that drives the change.

As with all ventures, this first step is the most important one; if you cannot pass the first step there is no point moving on to the next.

It's a bit like learning how to walk before you can run.

If you don't know how to use your feet and keep your balance, you are just going to trip and fall.

If you are not sure that you want to give up, you are just going to fail.

And probably rather quickly, wh ch means you will feel disappointed and upset even angry with yourself for failing. This will lead to frustration, which will fuel the bad habit, because you will blame yourself for failing to give up with thoughts like: "I failed", "I can't do this", "I knew it would be too hard", "There is no way I can give up even for a week," etc. and all the other pejorative things we say to ourselves. Because let's face it, we never say anything encouraging to ourselves like we might do to a friend who is trying to give up:

"Wow, you look great after not smoking for a week!"

"You did really well getting through that presentation at work today. No cigarettes even though you were nervous. You can do this!"

"I don't know how you managed to get through today without smoking, you're doing really well. Keep it up!"

No, instead we look to other people and sing their praises instead of our own.

If you've never encouraged yourself, try to start. It may feel awkward at first, but this is one of the good habits I want you to take on board and make part of your routine. Say one nice thing to yourself about yourself every day. Maybe in the morning before even getting out of bed or at the end of the day before drifting asleep. If that is too hard, think of 3 things/people you are grateful for or that make you happy.

The awkward feeling of complimenting yourself and feeling grateful for your life will gradually decrease after a week of doing this and it will break down your barriers of self-hate and self-criticism replacing them with self-respect and self-appreciation.

It is definitely worth starting something new for someone like you – you picked up this book, it means you can see your self worth, you want to make a change, ditch the bad habit, and START LIVING.

Important points:

- You're in charge
- Think about what you want
- Live according to your principles and no one else's
- Say something positive about yourself

START LIVING

2. WE'RE ALL DIFFERENT

Everybody but everybody is motivated differently. A different motivation for starting smoking, for continuing smoking and for stopping smoking. Just like we have a different motivation for why we enjoy going to work, for example:

because you love it

because of the paycheck

because of the cute guy/girl you get to see in the office

because the lunch is great

because you love the uniform

because of the travel perks

because it keeps you fit

because it pays for your cool clothes

Everyone is different.

So do not push yourself down a route just because someone says it works. It worked or works FOR THEM. You are an individual, find your own path. Base it on a general path that seems to fit your character and then tailor it to suit you.

We are all different. Even the way one person smokes is different from another.

We have heavy smokers, 40 cigarettes a day – where do they find the time! Then there are the

- social smokers
- nervous smokers ·
- stressed smokers
- I'm bored smokers
- if I stop I'll get fat smokers
- he smokes so I smoke smokers
- I love breaking the rules smokers
- serial quitters – you can put my book down, I'll give you a refund!
- stylish smokers
- eternal student smokers – usually rollies

Some have to give up "cold turkey"; others will simply cut down (a complete nightmare in the eyes of a heavy smoker) until they can wean themselves off.

Personally I just never said it was my last cigarette, I just said I'd only have my next one when I really wanted it and had nothing better to do – guess what, I've always found something better to do. But that's me; your way may be different. I have found "creating" to be much more rewarding than smoking. Smoking had become counter-intuitive to my desires in life. But I still made excuses at first, and you probably will too, such as: "Smoking gives me a break. I need it."

When you do eventually quit, you should still have breaks during work because you need them, but do something else like make a cup of tea and look through a paper or recipe book, do a yoga balancing pose or other completely different stuff like planting seeds, swing in the park outside in the sun. Just as long as it is a break. After a while you no longer take the same breaks at the same time as you used to. Breaks from work turn into "breaks" instead of "cigarette breaks".

I don't know about you but I am in pursuit of extending my life and of creating in my life. I don't want to be a passive being. What about all the people that invented all the cool stuff we can use like phones and cars? Did they just sit around like a sponge? They were people like you and me. In giving up bad habits my new mantra became: Get off your ass and do something!

Just because I want to achieve stuff and have a drive to do things, doesn't mean I don't lounge in front of some great films, everyone needs their downtime! And it doesn't mean you have to be like me. You will have your own drive and motivation for stopping smoking.

ROLE MODELS

Are you a role model?

Do you want to be a role model for your children?

I believe the next generation should be a better version of the one that went before. Whenever you read the news or talk to people, they tend to say we are failing as a "civilization". But really we are not, we are going from strength to strength and our children deal with much more than we did and our parents before us. They process a lot more information than we had to. I want my children to be better than me. It's like an old boss of mine used to say:

"I only hire people that are cleverer than me."

Our future generation should be cleverer than us.

How can you lead your team or teach your children if you are doing some pretty obviously stupid stuff? Like killing yourself and burning their holiday money all in the same go? Be the right kind of role model.

Maybe there is somebody *you* want to be like - think of 3 role models you may have.

Do any or all of them smoke?

Is smoking a characteristic you admire?

It might be your dream to be just like them. And do you know what, that's an achievement too. Do you want to be just like Mozart? Charles Dickens? James Dean? Bruce Lee? Angelina Jolie?

Why it can be helpful to have role models. Here are some examples:

- For having fun and getting the most out of your life: Jennifer Lawrence, she's a definite "I don't give a hoot about precast formulas, I'm good at what I do".

- For never saying die and looking good whilst you do it: Robert Downey Jr. Maybe in the 1990s you had him written off your list, then he resurrected himself like the phoenix and came back into the game even stronger than before playing such diverse characters as a lawyer to a superhero. He hit rock bottom, he gave up some pretty bad habits – this should give you hope – so you can too!

- For being happy and loving life: Mandy Ingber, another self-made lady. Her yoga sessions were and are just such a positive input into life. It's not real yoga it's a mix. So don't feel that you need to be a rubber bendy doll to do it, you don't. In fact I have lent out or recommended her stuff to friends – men mainly! Men who needed to get their bodies back into shape after a sedentary life or who wanted to stretch a little further literally.

We must also mention Angelina Jolie for constantly reinventing herself (but always looking the same) – hat off to her. A real kick-ass woman!

This list is not exhaustive, it's to prompt you to find your own role model if it will help you on your journey.

Here are some celebs that might help inspire you too

FORMER SMOKERS WHO QUIT

Jennifer Aniston, 2012

Matt Damon, 2004

Gwenth Paltrow, 2003

Courtney Cox, 1998

Ben Affleck, 2007

Ewan McGregor, 2009

Whoopi Goldberg, 2012

Christy Turlington Burns, 1995

There are plenty of them:

Just search "Celebrities who quit smoking" – some of them may shock you, but please note that they have all been pretty recent quitters.

Possible reasons for them quitting recently include:

1. Society is definitely making it harder to smoke, which works in your favor. There has been a monumental shift to anti-smoking compared with the pro-smoking days of the early 1900s.

2. People usually quit when they are over 30, at a life-changing moment in their life (e.g. approaching 40, about to have children, etc.).

3. It is no longer as cool to smoke as it was portrayed in the movies or adverts.

Important points:

- Find out what kind of a smoker you are – "light" wean off or "heavy" go cold turkey.
- Be a role model
- Find a role model

3.   REASONS & MOTIVATION

There are the usual, conventional reasons for stopping smoking that we are all aware of. Below is a list of some of these plus some alternative perspectives on why people should no longer smoke:

- it is bad for your health
- costs a lot of money
- save the planet
- stop premature aging
- no more bad breath
- stop feeling lethargic
- improve your red blood cell count
- speeds up the mental slowdown
- avoid impotence
- colic babies
- thousands of other health-related reasons
- it stinks...

But we already know all this.

And to be honest, when I smoked, none of the above seemed to be enough of a motivation to make me want to stop.

I enjoyed it, I loved it. It was something I liked doing. I smoked when I wanted and how many I wanted, end of story.

People often ask smokers if they have tried to give up , or "Why don't you give up?"

The simple answer from most smokers' point of view is:

"Because I don't want to."

Until YOU are ready to give up there is absolutely no point trying. (Yes I am making that one important point again: YOU HAVE TO WANT TO).

If you are not ready and do not want to give up smoking then don't. The list of reasons for stopping smoking could be as long as your arm, but if you don't really want to, none of them will have any effect on you. None of them will motivate you. And if you do stop, it will not be for good. You are most likely to relapse. The reason for stopping smoking has to be YOUR CHOICE.

I believe in quality of life and if you enjoy the habit it is better to be killed by something you enjoy than be miserable in life. Life is so short, you only live once, etc. you get the picture. So live it how you want to.

After all it is your body (just as long as you are not inflicting it upon others!)

If this is the path you have chosen, stop reading now and pick up this book again when you are ready.

You will of course have to put up with the bad breath and shortness of breath, plus a dull, aging complexion, never experience miraculously gaining lots more spare time, having more money in your bank account for stuff you want to buy and do. Instead you will be stuck with the same old habit. Boring, boring, boring.

If you have decided to stop (i.e. you chose this book, it was not given or bought for you), then read on. Stopping can be easier than you ever imagined.

A MAJOR CHANGE IN YOUR LIFE

There are two sides to this point:

1. **Instigate** a major change in your life:

In case scenario number 1, you INSTIGATE a change in your life. In this change you opt for a new way of life and smoking is part of your old way of life. When you stop smoking you will not have the psychological duress of quitting or giving up a habit, you are changing.

When you instigate a major change in your life, you will enjoy a new sense of freedom and a new high. The rush you get from learning something new, leaving draining habits behind and being someone you've always wanted to be is a real rush. It is like living as the main star in your own movie – except for it is real life. Your life.

This was my path. I was the instigator of change in my life. You can be the instigator of change in your life.

or

2. **Experience** a major change in your life:

In case scenario number 2, you may be experiencing a change in your life. You need to recognize when this change is taking place and jump on the bandwagon (then proceed as in point 1). These kinds of passive or unavoidable changes that you may not have been in control of or have control over, could include:

-   moving house
-   having a child
-   changing jobs
-   separation, etc.

Take advantage of a new situation. This is when old habits may be hard to squeeze in so squeeze them out. Make the most of this new change;

see it as an opportunity to get something more out of life. Exit your comfort zone because staying it will only bring you more of the same. Take the bull by the horns and ride it off into the sunset!

If nothing is about to change in your life then make it change (point 1). You may ask, how? Take up a sport, if you want change, move your legs. Why not try it out? Get moving physically; see if this move shifts your life. You'd be surprised with all the changes that follow one simple change in your life like joining the gym or local barre or dance class. Get out of your comfort zone, volunteer, leave your whining partner, go travelling, do something you would not ordinarily do. You have to make the change a shift in your life, in your routine.

Music really helps to motivate. Use it to lift up your mood or to energize your thoughts and body to make the change.

I personally bombarded myself with dozens of changes (yoga, martial arts, painting, DIY, woodwork, learning a new language, jogging, baking, gardening...) until I settled down to just the ones I really wanted to do and as a consequence I no longer had time for (or thought of) smoking.

If you tend to smoke mainly when you drink, no matter whether it is coffee or alcohol, then you must give up drinking first - that is essential.

Once you have accomplished this - read my book *How to give up drinking* - you will notice that you are already smoking a lot less or that you stop altogether as a natural consequence of no longer drinking.

You must not **deny** yourself any of the situations where you look forward to a "cigarette break" or some "quiet time", you should relocate them and have them at a different time, otherwise your pattern of habits linked with smoking will still be there, e.g. every time you turn up to your usual spot in the morning for a quick cigarette – this is a lot of people's favorite time before the rest of the family wakes up. You need to start your day off the right way with those 3 things you are happy or grateful for. Have some breakfast and do something you like for 20 minutes, e.g. a long shower when maybe you previously rushed, a longer walk in the fields with the dogs or a lie in! Many find meditating first thing in the morning helpful. This will enable you to focus on being calm and the breathing will reduce your physical cravings.

Redefine your mornings.

Change your routine, have breakfast as soon as you get up even if you do not want to, do it. Make a new habit, if having breakfast is too difficult then get ready (washed and dressed), make sure you do not have any time left to even think about smoking.

Every cigarette break has to be transformed into something new or completely ignored. The more days you spend without a cigarette between your fingers the less you will think about it and the more accustomed your body will become to being nicotine-free.

For the rest of this book I would love to not even mention the word "smoking" because it is no longer a part of your NEW LIFE. But that would be impractical.

Visualize life without smoking. See yourself as just you.

Now you are going to focus on doing something you have never had time to do. Buy and ride a motorbike, go to the gym, write a book, learn Dutch, knit a jumper, learn archery, travel to Thailand, start swimming classes, train as a hairdresser or beekeeper, bake cakes for school, help out at a charity store…. it does not matter what it is. Just as long as it is not boring old smoking.

MORE TIME

Below are some statistics to help you understand just how much time you are wasting by smoking and how much time you will be gaining when you no longer smoke.

Let's look at you heavy smokers first.

The calculations are based on an average of 10 minutes per cigarette, 20 cigarettes per day

20 x 10 = 200 minutes, which translates into 3 hours 20 minutes per day

1,400 minutes

23 hours and 20 minutes

You would gain **A WHOLE DAY per week**. Imagine what you could do in a whole day!! You don't even have to do anything you could just relax!

Cost

1 day	1 week	1 month	1 year
£10.00	£70.00	£280.00	£3,360.00
$5.60	$39.20	$156.80	$1,881.60

Time

1 day	1 week	1 month	1 year
200	1400	5600	67200
1,440	10,080	40,320	483,840
3 hr. 10 min	23 hr. 10 min	93 hr. 10 min	1,120 hr.
	almost 1 day	**almost 4 days**	**over 46 days**

Those of you smoking 20 cigarettes a day are smoking the equivalent of almost a month every year!!

You could go on holiday!

Maybe you can kind of shrug off wasting a small section of your day but when you look at what it accumulates to over the period of a year, it is a little more shocking.

20 cigarettes a day YOU LOSE AROUND ONE AND A HALF MONTHS EVERY YEAR!!!

Below is the example for those of you only smoking 10 cigarettes a day.

The calculations are based on an average of 10 minutes per cigarette, 10 cigarettes per day

10 x 10 = 100 minutes, which translates into 1 hour 40 minutes per day

11 hours and 40 minutes a week

Meaning you would be **gaining half a day per week, almost 2 days per month and over 23 days every year**

10 cigarettes a day

Cost

1 day	1 week	1 month	1 year
£5.00	£35.00	£140.00	£1,680.00
$2.80	$19.60	$78.40	$940.80

Time

1 day	1 week	1 month	1 year
100 mins	700 mins	2,800 mins	33,600 mins
1 hr. 40 min	11 hr. 40 min	46 hr. 40 min	560 hr.
	almost half a day	**almost 2 days**	**over 23 days**

Those of you smoking 10 cigarettes a day are smoking the equivalent of almost a month every year!!

You could go on holiday!

Maybe you can kind of shrug off wasting a small section of your day but when you look at what it accumulates to over the period of a year, it is a little more shocking.

Even with only 10 cigarettes a day YOU LOSE JUST SHORT OF A WHOLE MONTH EVERY YEAR!!!

Do not forget to look at how much money you save too (I did not work these out by accident) because monetary factors seem to be more important to us than our health. Just like it is a well-known fact that vanity is also a main reason for stopping: some women stop when they realize that the nicotine and tar are actually aging them prematurely[1].

The reason why you want to stop does not really matter, it is the result that counts.

IMPORTANT POINTS

- The greatest motivation of them all: A MAJOR CHANGE IN YOUR LIFE
- Instigate the change. Be the change
- Experience the change. Recognize a change
- Regain up to a month every year of lost time

---

[1] https://www.dermnetnz.org/topics/smoking-and-its-effects-on-the-skin

4. BE PREPARED

Now that you have decided that you *want* to stop smoking or rather that you do not want to smoke, that cigarettes no longer have a place in your life, no longer have a control over your bank account or your health, the rest is *really easy*.

Preparing yourself

I have heard people say they have written lists and sorted out schedules for when they were going to stop. Getting organized can be a good thing. It can be a period of time to adjust your head to the new situation. Just stopping though is far more effective. Just stopping does not give you the chance of thinking about it or making helpful rules like "just one cigarette at weekends" or "if I'm good for a week I can have one with my drink on Friday."

But you may need to schedule things in especially if you are "instigating a change" in your life. You may need to take some preparatory steps. Another possibility is a "rewards schedule". Well mapped out and planned rewards you can afford thanks to stopping smoking can be extremely motivating

Another point to bear in mind when you "prepare to stop" is exercise. If you do not want to put the pounds or kilos on after quitting, because you inevitably will because your metabolism will slow down, as nicotine speeds it up then start **exercising before you quit**. Add swimming, jogging, fast walking to your daily routine *before* you quit. You will notice that it actually helps you quit.

Or at least that you feel so bad after exercising with all the wheezing and coughing that you will want to quit!

PURGE YOUR MIND AND BODY

You have to take those essential steps of removing yourself from situations where you smoked and remove those situations or people out of your life. Be ruthless. This is **YOUR LIFE** we are talking about.

If there are people in your life who do not want to help you, it means they do not care about you and you might want to consider giving them up as well!

When I say "Be Prepared" I do not just mean getting your list of alternative routines ready and drawing up your reward planner. I mean be prepared mentally for the side effects. Some are good, some are bad.

Good physical effects

Everyone knows the physical part, but here is a quick overview just in case, plus it is also good to reinforce the positive effects of not smoking:

After 20 minutes

Your heart rate will begin to drop back toward a normal level.

After 2 hours

Your heart rate and blood pressure will be close to normal levels again. Your blood circulation will also start to improve. Nicotine withdrawal symptoms start.

After 12 hours

Carbon monoxide in your body decreases so the amount of oxygen in your blood increases to normal levels.

After 24 hours

Risk of coronary artery disease already begins to decline, as does the risk of having a heart attack.

After 48 hours

You get your old sense of smell and taste back – life just got a whole lot better!

After 3 days

You're nicotine free – well done!

After 2 to 3 weeks

Significant improvements in breathing, blood circulation and heart function. Lungs clearing, body regenerating and healing. No more REALLY BAD cravings.

After 1 to 9 months

Your body is better equipped to fight off infections and diseases. Your skin looks great.

After 1 year

Your risk of heart disease is lowered to half that of a smoker's.[2]

---

[2] www.healthline.com

But the ride is not all sunshine and roses. Here are some unpleasant things you may have to endure:

Unpleasant physical effects[3]

- intense cravings
- anxiety, tension, or frustration
- drowsiness or trouble sleeping
- increased appetite
- headaches
- nausea
- cramps
- sweating
- anxiety
- irritability
- depression
- bleeding gums

How to help alleviate these unpleasant symptoms:

Teeth + Gums

The last item on the list may surprise you. You may think it should be the other way around: healthier gums when you stop smoking. In essence they will be but initially, as soon as you stop smoking you may experience bleeding gums when you floss or brush. Because your circulation improves, the blood rushes back into them making them tender. To avoid this, you need to brush more and floss more, get them cleaned properly by your dentist or hygienist.

Look after your teeth; you do not want to end up with dentures or

---

[3] www.healthline.com

shrinking gums.

Watch out for sugary stuff that attacks your teeth like fruit, sweets, pop, etc. Brush your teeth after consuming sugary foods or drinks, even without toothpaste if you are not at home – do not make it a chore, make it a habit.

More vitamin C

You will also need more vitamin C, so you have to eat more fruit. Your body may crave it naturally or you may want comfort food in the form of junk food. If the latter applies to you, force yourself to add grapes, strawberries, blueberries, etc. to your diet - and do not come up with the excuse that fresh fruit is expensive because each cigarette was costing you the same price as a banana.

Skin

And you may also have breakouts in your skin - nice I know so much to look forward to!

But these will pass after a couple of months as your chemical levels and hormones rebalance in your body.

Depression

There is also the risk that if you give up you could get depressed. Your body could also go into shock since it used to the intake of nicotine. You will lose clarity and focus. These are all factors you need to consider in your "preparation phase". Decide if you are going to join a help group like the AA. Decide who you can call in a time of need. Get your safety net system in place before you stop smoking. I would like you to be able to deal with these side effects of giving up because they will not last forever and they should not be a reason for your relapsing.

In your work, like me, you may depend on being able to focus. I was very scared for the first few days when I could not focus (I had also given up caffeine and alcohol so my case may be different from yours) and I could only concentrate for 5 to 10 minutes at a time. I simply worked with it, taking breaks. After a week it got better and after a couple of months, I was back to normal again with even greater clarity, lucidity and focus than before. You might want to bear this in mind and take a week off work when you stop. This could tie in with your Major Change in your life and routine as well.

That is what I mean by "**Be Prepared**". I' is more than buying nicotine patches! You want to set yourself up to succeed as best as you possibly can.

Giving up can be a scary place to be but it is only temporary and it gets better, much better. The pros far outweigh the transitory setbacks you (or may not) experience at the beginning. I just want you to be aware of them, not to fear them, so you can be prepared.

Return to the idea of saying positive things to yourself, it would make a huge difference in your preparations. Affirm stopping as a positive step and these minor initial side effects will pass as your body detoxes.

Tell others you are stopping

You should tell those you live and work with that you are giving up. It is the decent thing to do – I did not want to tell anyone – I just kind of wanted it to be low profile, not having to face the questions of "How is it going?" or "I thought you gave up!" if I was caught having a *sly one*. That was my personal choice, which may also work for you.

But you really need to tell them because then they will understand when you lose your temper (seemingly for no reason) at the drop of a hat or when you thump your boss for looking at you the wrong way… yes your temper does get a little tethered due to the withdrawal symptoms. Unless you can lock yourself away in a cabin on top of a mountain for a month (good way to give up, by the way), you should tell your friends, colleagues and loved ones.

After your body has flushed out all the bad stuff, toxins, tar, nicotine, etc. and you have regained your focus, the rest of the journey is entirely up to you and your brain. Once you have physically purged yourself, it is the mental game, the habit of rolling, lighting and doing something with your hands that you will be battling. Do not worry; you can do it because YOU WANT TO.

You also need a TO DO LIST (whether it is written down or in your head), the one you drew up in your preparation stage of alternative routines. You could use it to help you in times of sheer and dire panic when your brain is no longer thinking clearly and your Dud Tyler side (see Fight Club movie) is taking over - kind of Jekyll and Hyde like - saying "Go on, just have one, you deserve it, you need it. Everything is failing, you can do this just have one you'll feel better". That's when you need your inspiring To DO LIST.

Your TO DO LIST is not what to do to give up; it is what you are going to do INSTEAD of smoking:

You may think you will feel better after having a sneaky cigarette, but there are other things you could do to feel *even better* and avoid the aftertaste of failure (let alone the ashtray aftertaste in your mouth) when you put that Jekyll and Hyde cigarette out.

List them. Get a sheet of paper out write a few down now.

Stuff to do to get rid of that burning sensation in your gut and chest that says "feed me nicotine" - give yourself a different kind of rush:

If you get the urge:

- run as far as you can
- drink water
- do 50 sit-ups
- scream really loud for as long as it takes
- listen to music really loud (maybe need headphones here so your neighbors don't become your new problem)
- listen to really calm soothing music
- have a long hot bath no matter what time of the day it is
- eat celery – don't munch on junk food
- do yoga
- punch something, preferably a punch bag!
- sew, knit if your hands need to keep active
- do crosswords or Sudoku – just as long as this wasn't linked to a cigarette break!
- watch a movie to take your mind off it
- read a book to take your mind off it,
- get in your car and drive.
- go somewhere you ARE NOT ALLOWED to smoke – like a swimming pool, petrol station

Do any of these things straight away, do not let the beast inside tell you what to do. Bang it on the head before it can come up and be heard fully; scream it down or drown it out with loud music, run or exercise it out of your system until you are dripping with sweat.

To help tame the beast, plan things to look forward to:

- not just the annual holiday - something for you, or for you and your partner
- drop the kids off at your parent's house, have 1 or 2 nights away in a hotel, in a tent, in a camper van, at a friend's house.
- have a facial if that's what you like
- go to a sporting event
- visit the theatre
- do thai chi on the coast
- travel to distant shores
- experience other cultures and climates

Anything, the world is your oyster and try to make it once a month or at least once every two months.

If you are worried about how to pay for it, remember you are not spending money on cigarettes – or read my other guide on *How to save money* and you will soon find you have the extra £20, £50 or even £100 in your bank.

Remember YOU WANT TO STOP SMOKING

So fight the beast and do something else you want to do instead.

Try not to do the same thing twice in a row or you'll just create another dependency.

So many people replace it with food or sugary drinks, and then you will end up with a weight problem!

Do not create another bad habit

IMPORTANT POINTS

- Prepare your body and mind
- Be aware and have a safety net
- Tell others you are stopping
- Make a TO DO LIST to kill the craving beast in your chest
- Write a post-smoking bucket list

FINAL THOUGHTS

FIGHT EVERY SECOND

You must take every day, hour minute and second as it comes. Once you are over the physical dependencies it is plain sailing because it is up to you and you want to stop so that makes it a lot easier.

Sweat out every second and every minute of the actual "excretion" of nicotine from your body. Do not top it up otherwise you will be back to ground zero. You will be back at the start and your efforts and suffering will have been in vain

Once you have stopped, do not procrastinate on the next part:

Start living.

Because you are not sure if you should just go out and do what you want to do in life, you risk inviting in procrastination or "pencil sharpening" as I like to refer to it.

Do not put off living life to the full, seizing the day, now that you have gained so much more time because you no longer smoke. I advise against doing the mundane chores in life. This newly found time is for fulfilling your dream, not cleaning out the cupboards, vacuuming or sweeping out the garage. Who cares if it is dirty or messy a little while longer? Do not waste this opportunity now that you have come so far.

Live your dream. Do what you want to do. What you do with that extra month in every year is supposed to be your reward for stopping. Make all your hard work and effort worthwhile and do something equally amazing with that month: travel the world, take a sabbatical, go on holiday with your family, the sky is the limit now you have all that extra time and money and good health.

In addition to having more time (and more money), you will have gained far more precious albeit less tangible things too, such as:

- more credibility in the eyes of your children

- gratifying rewards (learning a new skill like martial arts or a language or carpentry)

- self-respect

IN SUMMARY: IMPORTANT POINTS

- You decide. You're in charge of your life
- YOU WANT TO - you want to be the star in your life story
- Write a TO DO LIST of all the stuff to do in the event of a craving
- Motivation: your own rewards, role models, so much more time to live your dream
- Don't **replace** smoking, **forget** it

Because you do not want to be reminded of your habit by replacing it with something else, it does not mean that it will always be easy not to think about smoking every single day after you have given up. My advice would therefore be to keep a copy of this book in your bedside table or in your drawer.

Highlight the sections that really talk to you and reread these in your times of weakness. Go back and reread the reason why you wanted to give up and enjoy living a full and enriched life. Pull out that card and remind yourself of the dream you are aspiring to. The dream that is on the other side of you breaking this bad habit.

If you can quit smoking, you know you can achieve anything. This is just the first step.

Do not hide behind the habit, break through it. On the other side a whole life of opportunities and great stuff to do is just waiting for you.

Pursue self-fulfillment and self-furtherment. Positive thinking. Positive living. Be calm, focused and strong. If your intent is strong, nothing can stop you from succeeding.

Stop smoking. Start living.

ABOUT THE AUTHOR

Francesca Hepton was born (1973) and raised in the USA but she studied in Europe. She has an MA in Modern Languages (University of St. Andrews), Erasmus Diploma (University of Mirail, Toulouse) and a Diploma in Natural Healing; she is a yoga practitioner and qualified crystal and Reiki healer. She is a successful writer and illustrator of children's books, and wellness instructor.

Due to the personal circumstances in her life and driven by her love for her two sons, she decided to share her methods for effectively changing her life by writing the How to… series of books.

She is a firm believer in the pursuit of happiness and helping people fulfil their desires to be happy and succeed.

As a research member of the "How To" think-tank team. Her research focuses on the topics of self-belief and self-furtherment.

www.ingramcontent.com/pod-product-compliance
Lightning Source LLC
Chambersburg PA
CBHW060628030426
42337CB00018B/3247